AF584815

This book belongs to

This book is dedicated to
peace and kindness
– J.R.

THE FIRST EASTER

illustrated by JESS RACKLYEFT

PENGUIN BOOKS

Easter is a time of year when people all around the world celebrate hope and new life.

We have Easter egg hunts and
make special food and get together
with family and friends.
But do you know why?

A long time ago, in a country far away, a man called Jesus travelled to the big city.

He was there to spread his message of peace and goodwill.

We call this day Palm Sunday because the people cheered and waved palm leaves to welcome him.

They came to listen
and learn from Jesus.

He cared for the poor and
the sick, and taught people
about love and sharing.

One day, he gathered twelve of his friends
and told them how much he cared for everyone.

He told them that something very sad was going to happen and asked them to remember him whenever they shared a meal.

Not everyone in the city agreed
with the things Jesus said.
There were people who
wanted to hurt him.

When they came for Jesus,
his friends wanted to protect him,
but they were too scared . . .

. . . and Jesus died.

We call this day Good Friday, but why is it good if something so terrible happened?

Because that is not the end of the story . . .
This story has a happy ending.

Jesus' friends laid him in a tomb
and they were very sad.

But when they visited on the third day,
two angels appeared.

The angels told them, 'Don't be afraid! Jesus has risen!'

And it was true.
Jesus had risen from the dead!

His friends were filled with joy.

They ran to spread the good news - that there is always love, new life and hope, even in the most difficult times.

So that's why we celebrate
Easter with joy and happiness,
surrounded by the people we love.

That's why we share a meal . . .

. . . and give Easter eggs as a symbol of new life.

And that is the story of the first Easter.

The special foods, ceremonies and symbols connected with Easter vary across different communities and cultures. For nearly two thousand years, people around the world have commemorated the sacrifice that Jesus made and celebrated the hope represented by his resurrection. But now even many secular cultures gather with the people they love to celebrate hope, life and new beginnings during the Easter period.

PUFFIN BOOKS

UK | USA | Canada | Ireland | Australia
India | New Zealand | South Africa | China

Penguin Random House Australia is part of the Penguin Random House group of companies whose addresses can be found at global.penguinrandomhouse.com.

First published by Penguin, an imprint of Penguin Random House Australia Pty Ltd, in 2026

Design by Tony Palmer © Penguin Random House Australia Pty Ltd

Printed in China

Penguin Random House Australia uses papers that are natural and recyclable products, made from wood grown in sustainable forests. The logging and manufacture processes are expected to conform to the environmental regulations of the country of origin.

A catalogue record for this book is available from the National Library of Australia

ISBN 978 1 76135 243 0 (Hardback)

We at Penguin Random House Australia acknowledge that Aboriginal and Torres Strait Islander peoples are the Traditional Custodians and the first storytellers of the lands on which we live and work. We honour Aboriginal and Torres Strait Islander peoples' continuous connection to Country, waters, skies and communities. We celebrate Aboriginal and Torres Strait Islander stories, traditions and living cultures; and we pay our respects to Elders past and present.